The Angryman Standard

By

The Angryman

Table of Contents

Dedication

This is dedicated to all the angry men of the world. You no longer have to suffer in silence.

Acknowledgment

Gentlemen, Savages, Thugs, Barbarians, Geeks, Nerds, and Intellectuals. To all my supporters, fans, and followers. To all the angry men who have endured long enough and have no more need for sacrifice. To those of you who are sick of suffering in silence. To those who no longer want to merely survive but choose to win. This book is dedicated to you. May it bring you success in all your endeavors.

-AM

Foreword

All I ever wanted was to be happy. Most men do. If I had to guess, I would say I had your average run-of-the-mill childhood. Aside from my parents being divorced and being raised by my grandmother, I would say it was normal: Saturday morning cartoons, action figures, comic books, and Nintendo games—the hallmarks of any Gen Xer's childhood. Despite being raised mostly by a woman, I had plenty of male role models. My grandmother had 14 siblings, half of which consisted of brothers. In addition to that, my grandmother only had sons. So even when my father wasn't present (from time to time), my uncles would fill in the gaps, teaching me everything I needed to know about manhood. Some were cautionary tales meant to scare my male cousins and me from forfeiting our power. "Never put anything you own in your woman's name," my uncle would tell my cousin and me regularly. "You'll definitely regret it," he'd say. Others were examples of trials and tribulations that we witnessed our uncles endure at the hands of our vindictive aunts.

I remember vividly seeing my aunt shoving my two cousins into a hatchback car loaded with clothes and furniture. I was in elementary school, and my classroom had a window view of the school's parking lot. I remember wondering to myself, "Where is she going with all that stuff?" As my school bus approached my grandmother's house, I saw my uncle working on a car in the driveway. He was in between jobs then and would often do mechanic work to make money. I would later put together that his lack of employment sparked my aunt's sudden change of heart about her marital situation. It's funny how she had another change of heart after my uncle acquired his CDL and became a truck driver. I'll never forget the look on his face after I told him what I saw at school that day. The panic on his face as he rushed home to find out where she had run off with his children and possessions.

Through the men in my life, I learned the difference between how a man is treated when he's in a position of power as opposed to when he is not. Little did I know, our wonderful society was hard at work crafting a dark new future that would rob men of their power, leaving them with very little say-so, if any. It seems this was becoming a common trend. Looking at any average television sitcom, you see men being portrayed as ultra-sensitive, neutered, domesticated pets and as dull-witted, eager to please, and just happy to be in the presence of any woman. The women seemingly had absolute power. Able to abuse the men at will as the audience laugh track plays in the background as if the abuse of men is something to laugh at.

Even commercials portray husbands as mindless, knuckle-dragging cavemen who can't do something as simple as changing the settings on a glade air freshener. I'm not even joking. I'm sure you remember that commercial. The air freshener is sitting on the table, occasionally spaying a refreshing mist. The husband and his dog (man's best friend) watch in amazement at the new-fangled invention. Suddenly, his wife casually walks over and presses the button to make the mist spray prematurely. The man and the dog look at each other in confusion. Just imagine how insulted I was watching this gross mischaracterization of the male intellect. Especially since women only hold one out of five STEM-related patents.

Men are responsible for 97% of all the world's inventions. However, we are being portrayed as idiots who can't even work an air freshener. Can you imagine? Think of the little boys watching those sitcoms and commercials. Think of the message it sends to our potential scientists, technicians, engineers, and mathematicians. It's no wonder boys are being left behind. It's no wonder that men don't know how to be men anymore. With the increasing rate of out-of-wedlock births and the single-mother epidemic, what role models do boys have left? Couple this with the fact that most male spaces are growing smaller and smaller due to women's demands for inclusion. What's left are very few places a young man can feel comfortable being himself. Most would say, why is it necessary for men to have their own spaces? Why can't women be permitted to join the clubhouse? Well, it's simple. In today's climate, everything masculine has been thoroughly vilified. If men do not have exclusive spaces where they are free to be themselves and develop organically, unencumbered by the judgment and new age shaming tactics of a culture that desires to make every space female-friendly, where would a boy develop manhood?

I believe this type of alienation has contributed to most, if not all, of the developmental problems that boys face today. Just like the public school curriculum that seems to cater more to girls than boys, our entire society has become a hostile environment for men. This pseudo-power shift has created an imbalance in our society. One that has created a ripple effect that has set humankind on the path to destruction. I believe the only way to right this ship is to put men back at the helm. It does not take a rocket scientist to see that humankind was much more prosperous with men playing the role of captain. In this new age of wokeness, or whatever you would like to call it, men and women are more miserable than they've ever been in the history of the world. Mental illness is rampant, and the entire human race is suffering from some complex form of an identity crisis. I honestly believe this is a result of tampering with gender roles. More specifically, tampering with the roles and authority of men. Men are and have always been the leaders of our society. Men built the modern world, and men currently maintain it, doing the jobs that women will not do. To tamper with the men is to tamper with civilization itself. Men are tired of being marginalized and disrespected. Not only as a whole but as individuals as well. As bleak as all this may seem, I have a solution that will kill two birds with one stone. It is incumbent upon the men to regain their power, beginning with their household. A man's house is his castle, is it not?

The biggest problem is that men no longer know how to be men. And I am not talking about something as trivial as shaving or playing sports. I am talking about being in charge, being the head of their household, and not allowing women to run all over them. This is the major problem with society that I have identified. This is also true in the micro and the macro. But how did this happen? Men are protective in nature, and we try to accommodate women, given that they have always been the weaker of the two sexes. The only problem is that today, women may still be weaker physically, but they are not the weaker in terms of power. They have manipulated men on a mass scale. They have taken full advantage of our sensibilities and used our own nature against us. They play on our desire for justice by demanding equality while simultaneously capitalizing on the privileges that have always been afforded them for being the weaker of the two sexes. In other words, they want just as much power as the men without any accountability or responsibility. Equality plus female privilege tips the scales in favor of women. This type of foolishness has gone on long enough and needs to stop immediately. My solution is to put the power back into the hands of the men through a set of simple but effective standards. I believe that if men apply these standards, they will take back the reins of power in their homes, relationships, and the entire world.

Chapter 1:
Understanding Female Nature

"They tremble when we are in danger and weep when we die, but the tears are not for us, but for a father wasted, a son's breeding thrown away. They accuse us of treating them as a mere means to our pleasure, but how can so feeble and transient a folly as a man's selfish pleasure enslave a woman as the whole purpose of nature embodied in a woman can enslave a man?"

– George Bernard Shaw, Man and Superman

First and foremost, we must understand female nature and, more specifically, what drives female nature. Hypergamy, colloquially referred to as marrying up, is a term used in social science that refers to the practice of a woman marrying a man of a higher caste or social status than herself. Hypogamy typically refers to the inverse occurring, marrying a man of lower social class or status. Both terms were coined in India in the 19th century while translating classical Hindu law books, which use the Sanskrit terms for the two concepts. Forms of hypergamy have been practiced throughout history, including in India, Imperial China, ancient Greece, the Ottoman Empire, feudal Europe, and the United States. Today, most people marry their approximate social equals, and in much of the world, hypergamy is in slow decline. For example, it is becoming less common for women to marry older men. However, even in more progressive societies, it is generally accepted that young women often partner with powerful older men.

Studies of heterosexual mate selection in dozens of countries around the world found men and women report prioritizing different traits when it comes to choosing a mate, with men tending to prefer women who are young and attractive and women tending to prefer men who are rich, well educated, ambitious, and attractive. Evolutionary psychologists contend this is an inherent sex difference arising out of sexual selection, with men driven to seek women who will give birth to healthy babies and women driven to seek men who

2

will provide the necessary resources for the family's survival.

However, social learning theorists say women value men with higher earning capacity because women's ability to earn is constrained by their so-called "disadvantaged" status in a male-dominated society. I'm of the opinion that it is the former and not the latter. Women choose men who are rich and handsome. If he's not handsome, they'll settle for rich. These same social learning theorists also argue that as societies shift towards becoming more gender-equal, women's mate selection preferences will also shift. I disagree. I can think of quite a few men who made the mistake of believing that because we live in a more "progressive" society, women will tamp down their hypergamous nature and somehow circumvent thousands of years of bio evolution. It's unsurprising that men think this way with the emergence of pop culture movies that display the proverbial "nice guy" getting the girl.

In fact, in the early 2000s, there was an explosion of movies where the lovable geek/misunderstood nerd miraculously won the heart of the most popular girl in school. Or, as Dr. Warren Farrell would call them, the genetic celebrity. And he did it without changing anything about his looks, mannerisms, or social status. She accepted him for who he was and not what he had or what he could do for her. This is fiction. That very thinking has led to countless men being rejected consistently. This is how you create an incel.

Now, of course, there's always some obscure research that supports the more progressive theory, such as a 2012 analysis of a survey of 1,953 people in 37 countries, which found that the more gender-equal the country, the more likely the male and female respondent would report seeking the same qualities as each other than different ones. However, in 1989, Townsend surveyed medical students regarding how the availability of marriage partners changed as their educational careers advanced. 85% of the women indicated that as their status increases, their pool of acceptable partners decreases. In contrast, 90% of men felt as their pool of acceptable partners increases, their status increases.

In 2008, Paul argued that based on mathematical models, human female hypergamy occurs because women have greater loss mating opportunity costs from monogamous mating, given their slower reproductive rate and limited fertility window, and thus must be compensated for this cost of marriage. Marriage reduces the overall genetic quality of her offspring by precluding the possibility of impregnation by a genetically higher quality male, albeit without his parental investment. However, this reduction may be compensated by greater levels of paternal parental investment by her genetically lower-quality husband.

Loosely translated, the women would choose the readily available genetically lower-quality male. Because of his stability, he was a more suitable choice for fatherhood, especially for a woman seeking provision and security through marriage and motherhood. Due to his subordinate nature and lower social standing, it was almost guaranteed that he would never leave, thus ensuring that her children would always have a father and she would be taken care of for the rest of her life. Plus, there's the bonus of being able to boss him around due to his lower social status. A prime example of this is Bill Cosby's 1980s sitcom, "The Cosby Show," where Clair would constantly crack jokes about Cliff's looks while Cliff constantly praised hers. It's obvious she picked Heathcliff for stability, not looks. Remember when she told Cliff that she would have married a handsome man with a smaller nose if she had listened to her mother?

Choosing a genetically higher-quality male would be a timely and difficult endeavor, one that has no guarantee due to the options available to said male. After all, Mother Nature waits for no one, and that biological clock is always ticking. Plus, you can forget about bossing this one around. Men with options are harder to control. Despite this frustrating trade-off, the women of today have found an interesting solution. Instead of choosing one or the other, why not have both? After all, if feminism has taught women anything, it's taught them that they can have it all. Today, women use their youth to attract and mate with a genetically higher-quality male without getting married.

Why bother marrying a male who is unsuitable for marriage/fatherhood? Then, later in life, after their beauty fades, they pursue the genetically lower-quality male that is suitable for marriage/fatherhood. So basically, they're able to bear children with the man they want and then have the man they don't want raise said children and secure her lifestyle. It's called "Alpha Fucks, Beta Bucks." The best of both worlds. Women who engage in this type of behavior must be avoided at all costs. As horrible as this all sounds, you must understand that this is female nature. Alpha Fucks, Beta Bucks is an extremely deformed, dysfunctional form of hypergamy, but it is hypergamy, nevertheless. Remember, women will always search for the bigger, better deal. The only way to nullify this is to be the bigger, better deal.

An empirical study examined the mate preferences of subscribers to a computer dating service in Israel with a highly skewed sex ratio of

646 men for 1000 women. Despite this skewed sex ratio, they found that women, on average, express greater hypergamous selectivity on education and socioeconomic status. They prefer mates who are superior to them in these traits. To quote the late, great Patrice O'Neal. "I'm better than you!" At the same time, men express a desire for an analog of hypergamy based on physical attractiveness. They desire a mate who ranks higher on the physical attractiveness scale than they do.

In the spaces where I congregate and men debate, hypergamy is spoken of like it's a boogie man. I can see why men detest the concept, as it displays the self-serving nature of female behavior. But take one moment to think about it objectively, and you might find that this behavior they view as a strength can also be a weakness. Feminist analysis of hypergamy says the practice needs to be understood in the context of a patriarchal system. Understand that the practice of female hypergamy can only exist in a system where men achieve more, a system where men rule. This hints at how female nature can be used to your advantage.

Men choose attractive partners because they can, and women choose partners with material resources because they desire a stable, secure, comfortable life. And they will fight tooth and nail to achieve it. This works for you and not against you. Do you plan on achieving more, or do you plan on achieving less? I, for one, plan on achieving more. Make no mistake (and this MUST be said): I am not pursuing success solely for the acquisition of women. That would be a foolish endeavor. I am pursuing success for the achievement of my own glorious purpose. And I suggest you do the same. Women are a side effect—a bonus. So don't mistake the purpose of pursuing success. The point is you don't have to defeat hypergamy.

This reminds me of a story. Two men are hiking in the woods and come upon a huge grizzly bear rearing up. The first guy slowly slides off his backpack in preparation to make a break for it. The second guy says, "What do you think you're doing? We can't outrun a grizzly bear." The first guy says, 'I don't have to outrun the grizzly bear. I just have to outrun you." Moral of the story. You don't have to achieve the impossible, like outrunning a grizzly bear. You just have to be better than the guy next to you. Achieve that, and hypergamy will always work in your favor.[1]

Now that we understand hypergamy, the main driving force that motivates all women (which, put simply, is all about money/resources/security), let's delve into the most confusing aspect of female nature as it pertains to mating and dating, namely, why she loves the bad boy and hates the nice guy.

A riddle has puzzled young men of every generation, even to this day. Well, first, we need to understand the counter-intuitive mind of the female. For many of us, females have always been confusing, and it can be difficult to understand how they think. The way they communicate on several levels definitely differs a lot from men. But I'll take it one step further. You see, there are aspects of female nature that nobody ever took the

---

[1] What is HYPERGAMY? What does HYPERGAMY mean? HYPERGAMY meaning, definition ... noun: the action of marrying or forming a sexual relationship with a person of a superior sociological or educational background.

time to teach us when we were young. These cold truths about women's psychology may seem crazy to say out loud because no one really talks about them. And even women themselves aren't aware of it. Sure, there are a few PUA guys and Red Pill dudes who have attempted to tackle the subject. However, in my opinion, I think they miss the subtle nuance of this behavior. But don't worry. That's what I'm here for. So, let's break down what you need to know before you unwittingly set yourself up for failure in dating and relationships. I remember a long time ago, when I was in my early teens, I was interested in a girl named Bethany. And no, that's not her actual name.

Do you really think I would give some chick from back in the day that type of shine? Please. Anyway. We were in the same grade but didn't have any classes together. I would see her in the halls between classes from time to time. From the first day I laid eyes on this chick, I was done. A real sucker-for-love type, dude. You know how some people say they had butterflies in their stomach?

Well, my butterflies were the size of pterodactyls. I would sit in class and daydream about her, thinking about what it would be like if she was my girlfriend, holding hands as I walked her to class, trading love letters and kissing those beautiful lips.

Every love song on the radio made me think of her. In my immature juvenile mind, all would be right with the world if I could just get this one girl. I can admit now that I was obsessed with her. It got to the point where I was thinking about her every day. I felt like I was going crazy.

But I didn't show it. Sometimes, we would even make eye contact, but I would casually look away. Eventually, we both ended up having mutual friends, and I felt an attraction whenever we were around each other. She seemed to be giving off vibes as if I had a shot. But I barely spoke to her. Expressing my feelings was a daunting task. The fear of rejection was almost crippling. I knew I had to do something, but I didn't know what. Around that time, the school had a book fair. So, I decided one Friday I was going to buy her some flowers and a large teddy bear. I would present her with the gifts and confess my feelings. After all, that's how the guys did it on TV and in those sappy love stories. I would let it all out and tell her I had a crush on her, and the gifts would be my grand gesture. So that's what I did. I caught her after school right before she got on the bus. "Hey, Bethany, I got these for you."

"Oh my god. Thank you. This teddy bear is so cute."

"Yeah. I wanted to give these to you because I think you're kind of fly."

Just then, the bus driver started rushing her to get on the bus. She smiled and said, "I'll see you Monday," and got on her bus. At that moment, I felt a huge sigh of relief, like I had just gotten a huge weight off my shoulders. I kicked myself for not getting her phone number right then. We could've spent the entire weekend chatting. But instead, I spent the whole weekend thinking about my soon-to-be new relationship. Because I had finally told her how I felt, I knew Monday she would be my girl. And yet, when Monday came, I noticed the vibe between us had changed. And not in a good way. Now, she wasn't looking my way in the hall. No more random glances. She didn't seem interested in the least. It was like she was avoiding me. Something had changed.

See, I was young and naive enough to think that once I finally confessed my feelings to her, she would immediately feel the same way or at least be pushed in that direction. But instead, I got almost the opposite response. It was almost like once I told her how I felt, she started pulling away like it did more harm than good. My chances with her seemed bleak. After an entire day of basically being ignored, I confronted her after school.

"Hey. I know Friday you were in a rush to get on the bus, but I was wondering if I could get your number so I can call you?"

"Yeah. I was in a rush, but. Look, I'm sorry, you're a cool guy, and it was really sweet of you to give me those gifts, but I only like you as a friend."

Those infamous words every guy on the planet hates to hear. She tried to friend-zone me. I felt super let down and frustrated, obviously. And more than that, I felt confused. I mean, before giving her those gifts and telling her how I felt, I could have sworn that she was at least feeling me a little bit. She would give me these flirty glances as I passed her in the hallway. Now, she barely looked my way. It didn't make much sense to me back then since I was still inexperienced with girls. But that was the first time I vividly remember observing this phenomenon. And over the years since then, it's only become clearer to me as I've been around more and more diverse social situations.

You see, women want a guy that they deem as a win. Meaning she must work to get him. As Patrice said, every woman wants a winner, a guy that's better than them. And by the mere act of buying gifts and professing my love, I appeared less than her. Remember, their hypergamous nature makes them desire things they can't easily attain. It's why they love movies like Cinderella, where the handsome prince who could have any girl ends up with poor Cinderella.

Remember how much Cinderella had to do to impress the prince. She didn't show up to the ball in her rags. She had to have a fairy godmother use magic to step her game up. I thought giving Bethany gifts would make her feel special, showing her just how special I thought she was. And I wasn't wrong about women wanting to feel special. But women only want to feel special from a guy they deem a win. So, she looks at your behaviors. She wants to feel that attention from a guy who has other options—guys who are less needy, stronger, and more independent. The truth is, she wanted a winner.

Knowing what I know now, she probably was interested in me. Those sneaky glances my way indicated as much. But there was one thing I didn't know. It was my original behavior that inspired her interest in the first place. By casually looking away when our eyes met, it made me seem indifferent and aloof. By not telling her my feelings, I was a mystery to be solved. Gaining my interest would be a challenge. The moment I told her how I felt.

And then I bought her those goofy gifts (facepalm). I immediately killed the mystery and ultimately removed the challenge of her pursuing me. Why do you think women love romance novels? It's the buildup—the anticipation of not knowing what will happen next. If you put the outcome on the cover, they'd never read the book. Laying your cards out on the table and telling her how you feel is like spoiling the end of a good mystery. And like anyone who loves a good mystery, women will resent you for this.

Remember that women are all about nonverbal communication. Whether knowingly or unknowingly. And showering a woman with gifts and compliments upon initially meeting them communicates to them that you are low value. Nice guys don't understand this simply because it's counter-intuitive. The nice guy believes by telling her she's beautiful, making kind gestures, and buying her things, he's displaying value. And in a logical world, he would be right. But the female mind perceives a guy who doesn't believe he's enough, so he must do all kinds of extra things to supplement what he is lacking. On the other hand, the Bad Boy, whom she perceives as the cool guy, the winner that she really wants, won't be so quick to give gifts or compliments. He's not too invested in anyone because he knows he'll be just fine without her.

See, that's who a woman wants. You see, the bad boy is typically more selfish and self-absorbed, which is why he's not too invested. Truthfully, he's not really focused on her. Again, this is counter-intuitive because women tend to like neglectful guys. The female mind perceives this as strength and independence. "He must be a winner because he doesn't need me." This gives her a challenge. An endless game of, "I'm going to prove to him he needs me, or I'm going to change him."

When you go the nice guy route, it feels to her like you're putting her on a pedestal. And contrary to what they say, women don't want that from a guy. Women flee from men who try to worship them. The truth is girls are much more receptive to guys when it feels like she's doing the chasing.

18

After everything's said and done, she got a man who could've had any woman he wanted. Again, it makes her feel special. What she doesn't want is to feel like you're chasing her too desperately because you put all your eggs in one basket. No girl fantasizes about a guy who makes a big deal about how pretty she is and behaves like he is so lucky to have her. Instead, she fantasizes about landing the guy who's almost too good for her. Don't you get it? She doesn't want admiration from a man. She is searching for a man worthy of her admiration.

Now, I want to add some nuance here. I'm not saying you should never show a woman you're attracted to her. I'm saying don't show your interest in a low-value way. You must always come from a position of power. You're in the driver's seat. What you must learn is how to express interest using nonverbal communication. This way, she knows, but she doesn't truly know. It's like catching a cat's attention with a laser pointer.

You point it at the wall and wait for the cat to see it. Then, you click it off or move it to another wall. Once the cat's curiosity is peaked, you keep it moving. You never allow the cat to possess it or know what it is. Sure, you want her to feel flattered by giving her the impression that you're interested. But what you don't want to do is make her feel like she already has you. Never give her the certainty that she already knows completely where your head is.

Her knowing with 100% transparency, your true desires and feelings will immediately remove all mystery. Think back to our analogy about Cinderella. Those movies never show the prince's back story or his inner dialog. That way, he's more mysterious. I know some of these concepts seem illogical or even ridiculous. But like Everett (played by George Clooney) said in the movie Brother Where Art Thou, "It's a fool who looks for logic in the chambers of the human heart."

I remember one girlfriend I had at 14 years old. A gorgeous girl who I pulled by accident. I saw her at a social event, and she immediately caught my eye. I leaned over to a friend of mine and told him how fine she was and how I would love to get with that. Little did I know, my friend knew her. He promptly told her what I said (against my wishes), which led to me getting her phone number. I'm still shocked it played out that way. After about a week of talking with her over the phone, I realized how much of a ding-bat she was. This girl had movie-star beauty but was boring as hell.

Eventually, I got so tired of her that I snapped. I told her I was done with her and never wanted to talk to her again. Then I banged the line, which meant I hung up on her. To my surprise, she called right back, asking what she had done wrong. I hung up again because I really was done with her. I didn't care how good she looked. What amazed me was that no matter how many times I hung up, she kept calling back. It was at that moment I finally understood what I had done wrong with Bethany a couple of years prior. Women don't want to be chased; they want to do the chasing. The only problem is getting them to chase you.

See, they'll never chase you if you're a nice guy. At least not while they're young and desirable.

Sure, they'll chase you after they hit the wall, but that's only because they're all out of options. This is the reason why Bethany tried to friend-zone me. She was attracted to me, but I ruined it for her by displaying low value. By attempting to keep me in the friend zone, she could keep her options open for a guy whom she perceives as a winner. If that guy didn't come along, she could always fall back on me for her guy needs. At least, she thought. Date for the prom, shoulder to cry on, date to make other guys jealous, etc.

Everything except boyfriend benefits like affection. This is the reason a lot of you guys are getting Facebook messages from chicks who friend-zoned you in high school. It's because they messed up with the guy they thought was a winner. Some never found a winner. I never allowed myself to be friend-zoned, but you get the idea of what I'm saying. Never allow a woman you have a romantic attraction for to friend-zone you. To her, you're just a boyfriend in a glass case. "In case of emergency, break the glass."

Never be a nice guy. But don't look at yourself as the bad boy, either. You're simply adjusting your approach to dating by considering her female nature and her tendency to get turned off by guys who make things too easy for her—guys who put her on a pedestal and chase her instead of letting her chase him. When I finally learned this cold truth of female nature at the age of 14, it felt like a bitter realization, almost like getting a hard dose of reality. But now, I've completely accepted instead of harboring resentment.

The truth is you can never change female nature. And you can never truly control it. Female nature is like fire. You can harness its power. You can use it to keep warm and cook your meals. It can bring you pleasure and help you build. But as the old saying goes, "Play with fire, and you'll get burned." Even worse, in some cases, you might get killed. And hell hath no fury, gentlemen.

Chapter 2:
The Vetting Process

"They say you judge a man by his wife, his car, and his shoes. Those three things will tell you everything you need to know about a man."

– Jerry Seinfeld

To all the young men reading this, I want you to do me a favor. Imagine you had all the money in the world. Picture yourself going to the car dealership of your choice. The salesman greets you and asks what type of car you want. Keep in mind that money is no object, so you can pretty much get anything you want with all the features and customizations you desire. Imagine the type of car you would get. I bet you have it pictured in your head. You can see it, can't you? All the way down to the color stitching on the interior seats. I bet if I asked you to describe it, you could rattle it off without even thinking about it. It's easy because you've probably dreamed about it your entire life.

However, if I were to ask you to tell me what type of woman you want, most of you wouldn't even have an answer outside of the obvious aesthetics. Imagine a guy who picks a car because the color is pretty.

It's funny how our male minds work. I'm certain you can give me every detail about that car but very little about the woman, even though you're probably using the car to impress and get the woman. This is very interesting since the woman will certainly give you more problems than the car ever will. At least with the car, you can get an extended warranty. Maybe ask one of your friends for the number of a good mechanic.

Nevertheless, I find it troubling that we take more time and care to vet something as transitory as a vehicle than we do when it comes to our women. After all, a car can't ruin your life. Correction: a car can't plot and plan to ruin your life. Far too often, guys come to ruin because they hooked up with some random chick without ever taking the time to look under the hood (as a sidebar, I know you ladies reading this are just loving the analogy). Instead, the average guy spots a pretty, shining new car and just hops in for a joy ride. Never take the time to inspect the car, check the fax (I mean Carfax), or even ask who the previous owner was (context ladies, context).

I shouldn't have to explain why this can be dangerous. At the very least, you could make the mistake of getting the wrong woman pregnant. And boom, there go the next 18 years of your life. And 18 is the short number, depending on if they go to college. No gentlemen. The vetting process is the most important step and should be employed every time you deal with a woman. I don't care if it's just a one-night stand. Too much hangs in the balance. Pun intended. So, in this section, I've decided to give you guys a few red flags to watch out for when you first meet any woman. These are red flags that come from research, advice, and experience. These warnings had served me well, saved me when I took heed to them, and haunted me when I ignored them.

Daddy Issues

Look out for a woman who has emotional baggage and "daddy issues." If she can't even get along with her father—the man who raised her—how do you expect her to get along with you? Women who don't have a relationship with their fathers are a red flag. The father-daughter dynamic is crucial because this is how she will learn to relate to men. Depending on how her mother and father interact, she will learn to value or hate men.

Her relationship with her father from childhood to adulthood will show her she can trust men and have confidence in their ability to lead. A good friend of mine always said, "Sons have the ability to outgrow their mothers, but daughters never outgrow their fathers." I couldn't agree more.

We have the wedding tradition of the father walking the bride down the aisle because he's handing her off to the man she will marry. A father passes down the responsibility of protecting, providing, and leading his daughter to another man. That is how women set the standards of what they look for in a suitable partner. It's based on their relationship with their father. Those who don't have a good relationship with their fathers tend to be rudderless in the dating pool. Or should I say, 'dating ocean'?

They neither know how to pick a good man nor maintain a decent relationship. This will cause enormous problems for you. While it is true that women seek validation from men, if their relationship with their father is bad, they may seek your validation through negativity, acting out for attention. The worst part is that she will be unable to accept any type of validation you give her. No matter what you do for her, she will always draw parallels between your relationship and the one with her father. There will always be that 'gap' in the relationship. Ultimately, you'll be paying for the sins of her father.

Trust Issues

If she grew up watching her mother fail to trust her father, she would do the same with every man in her life. Trust issues will become a significant part of your relationship. It will start subtly and then become a significant problem. She will start by asking questions like, "Where are you going,

28

babe?" which will then turn into "Who are you going with?"

This will become a significant problem, especially if you comply and answer this invasive line of questioning. You must understand that answering those types of questions puts you in a subordinate position, ultimately creating an illusion of control.

It will start subtly and then move on to interrogative questions. When she's not satisfied with your answers, she will then ask you to prove your innocence in some ridiculous way, like allowing her to go through your phone. She will begin keeping track of your whereabouts at all times and have you checking in like she's your probation officer. If you try to set boundaries, she will gaslight you into believing that her behavior is a normal part of relationships—as if grown-ass men are obligated to tell their women where they are, at all times, like children. She may even start an argument to condition you into compliance. Some men give in and comply just to avoid the stress of an argument.

On the flip side, she has plenty of boundaries for you. Remember? She educated you from day one on what you can and cannot do with her, how you can't come to her place until she gets to know you better, and not call her house after a particular hour. Or some ridiculous 90-day rule she learned from some zoot suit-wearing has-been comedian turned talk show host with a goofy 70s mustache. And you can forget about going through her phone. *It ain't happening, captain.* And you can forget about looking through her phone.

Don't get me wrong. She can make all the rules she wants. She's a grown woman, and she has that right. But you're a grown man, and you have the same right. There's nothing wrong with healthy boundaries, but never let anyone give you rules when they don't respect yours. The bottom line is if she can't trust you, she shouldn't be with you. It's not your job to cater to all her insecurities.

Stonewalling

If she stonewalls you, that's a red flag. Stonewalling is when you're trying to converse with her. Instead of taking the conversation seriously, she refuses to engage with you. Instead, she will pretend she is busy with something just to avoid the conversation. Women do this for a multitude of reasons. It's usually because she did something you disliked or disagreed with, and she's trying to avoid being wrong. Stonewalling makes it difficult for you to set boundaries. How can you tell her your boundaries if she doesn't take the conversation seriously? Or worse—if she's flat-out ignoring you?

Stonewalling is an effective way to avoid accountability. If she has a habit of doing this, it means she doesn't take you seriously. She doesn't view you as the one who has control of the relationship. In other words, she does not *respect* you. As a result, she will dismiss your concerns and pay no heed to what you tell her. For example, suppose you encounter a problem in the relationship. In that case, she will ignore it and pay no attention to how you feel about the problem.

This is because she wants you to know that she is the one who has control. The only issues of any importance are the ones she deems to be significant. She is the one who "wears the pants in the relationship." In other words, she wants you to give in to her demands and live life as she wants you to. These types of women will use all sorts of manipulative tactics to achieve this goal, things like the "silent" treatment or gaslighting. They will relentlessly display this behavior until you give in to them. Women like this must be avoided at all costs.

She Can't Take "No" for an Answer

The word " No " is the most powerful word in the English language when you're dealing with women is the word "No." The only problem is she can't take "no" for an answer. Everything must go her way. She will do everything in her power to control your actions. Especially If she knows you're madly in love with her, she will emotionally blackmail you. You will often hear things like, "If you really loved me, you would do this for me." You will start questioning yourself. You'll think, "Am I the one being unreasonable?" but let me tell you, no, you're not.

You have boundaries that are not being respected. You know the answer to this question—*she doesn't respect you.* You're not unreasonable for asking your woman to respect your boundaries and rules. If you feel a certain way, there's a reason for that. Always go with your first mind. It doesn't matter if she wants everything to go her way. She's an adult, not a child.

I had a friend who broke up with a needy girl, and for months, she stalked him. She couldn't believe it was over and that he didn't want to be with her anymore. She couldn't take "no" for an answer. She even pretended to throw herself down a flight of stairs. You're probably thinking, "Omg." Trust me, it's not as bad as it sounds. She pretty much rolled slowly down the steps, slid down the last three, and began to moan quietly. It was so ridiculous it looked like something out of a Saturday Night Live skit. Women believe that just because they are women, men will fall to their knees and worship them. Whenever a guy is fed up with a chick, they are shocked to find that he doesn't want her in his life, no matter how "pretty" she is. At that point, looks are irrelevant. Learn to say no. Learn to say it often. And never date a woman who has a problem with that.

Anger Issues

A woman with anger issues is a major red flag. This type of woman will never listen to a word you say once she's turned up. Instead, she will throw tantrums, curse you out in public or maybe even get physically violent. She's emotionally manipulative and dangerous because her actions are too unpredictable. Women like this can cut deep. Your hopes, dreams, secrets, etc., are all fair game. Nothing is off the table. Things you've told her that you've never told anyone else *will* come up in a heated argument.

Your past will also be used against you. Remember when you did XYZ on so-and-so day? You did this and that for an ex-girlfriend but not for her, so you don't love her as much as you loved your ex. If you don't earn as much as your friends or men she knows, she will rub it in your face. If she earns more than you, you're not considered "man enough."

She will purposely use things against you to hurt you. Then, in a moment of anger, she will do everything she can to break you. *You aren't good enough; you are not "man" enough. You are not worth her love and attention. You are worthless compared to other men.*

Nothing Is Her Fault

There's a reason there are so many jokes about wives being "right" all the time. You even see it in countless television sitcoms. The problem is that life isn't a joke or a television sitcom. Her thinking she's right all the time and constantly blaming you for every little thing significantly impacts your mental health and general peace of mind. How many times have you come home to your chick starting a fight over something stupid or trivial?

When you try to reason with her and logically solve the situation, she gets even angrier. She continues her borage of bullshit until you give in to her and let her win because you just want the arguing to end. This is a huge mistake, but it's also the reason wives believe they're always right. It's a form of emotional bullying. They apply the pressure until you submit. *It's their version of physical abuse. The only difference is they're allowed to get away with it.* Eventually, you'll find yourself apologizing for something you didn't do.

The funny thing is, she will never apologize to you for anything she does. Think about it. When has a woman ever apologized to you? How can she if she's NEVER wrong? This has been the central theme in modern Western society. Everything is always the man's fault. It's called "The Duluth Model," which is basically a man-hating ideology dreamt up by a bunch of man-hating feminists on their never-ending mission to destroy the Patriarchy and take over the world. *I'm not joking.* The fact is that men built and ruled the world, which led them to the assumption that anything wrong with the world is inevitably men's fault. And all men must pay for any perceived unhappiness that women experience.

Ridiculous, I know, but this is, in a nutshell, what they believe. Women feel entitled because they believe they are inherently better than men. And if given the opportunity to rule the world, it would be a much better place. There would be no wars, homelessness wouldn't exist, world hunger would end, and blah blah blah. It would be a kinder place filled with sunshine, rainbows, and fairy dust compared to the evil, war-ridden world of man. This fanciful thought gives them a sense of empowerment and self-righteousness, which puts the pompous male ego to shame. However, this is a severe contradiction, considering that their model of strength and empowerment is a juvenile impersonation of powerful men. How can you condemn the actions of man while simultaneously mimicking him in a desperate attempt to appear powerful based upon the standard that men set? Put simply, if a man is a ruler you use to measure your ambitions of power, then his wrong is your wrong. Being a different gender doesn't change that.

This is why the Duluth Model is bullshit. A man wanting to dominate his wife with his god-given physical strength is no different than a woman dominating her husband with her god-given emotional prowess. An emotional argument leaves men at a disadvantage, just like a physical fight does to a woman.

It's not her fault; nothing is ever her fault. Everything wrong with the relationship depends on your behavior with her; it depends on whether you can read her mind or not. This is the equivalent of a man abusing his wife because dinner wasn't ready when he got home and him having the nerve to say, "Look what you made me do."

A friend of mine dated a girl who would never admit her faults. Finally, when he was breaking up with her, he said, "Look. I know I have made mistakes in the relationship, and I apologize, but can you please see that you've also done me wrong? She told him that she wasn't at fault because he hurt her more and the "amount of damage" he caused her was "inexcusable." This is emotional abuse. Avoid it at all costs.

She Flips In a Matter of Seconds

She goes from zero to a hundred real quick. You have to walk on eggshells around her because you never know what might set her off. She's a ticking time bomb. One moment, she's the sweetest thing in the world and can't get enough of you, walking around singing Toni Braxton's "I Love Me Some Him." Next thing you know, she'll make you feel like a worthless piece of shit.

I had a friend who was a barber. Often, we would hang out in the barbershop after hours. Sometimes two and three hours after the shop was closed. One day, he said to me, "I guess I better get on the road and make this forty-minute drive." I remember saying to him if you live forty minutes away, why on earth are you hanging out with me two hours after the shop closed?

He said, "Honestly, I'm avoiding my wife." He told me that he dreaded going home. He said not only does he hang out at the shop two hours after closing, but even after his forty-minute drive home, he would sit in the garage for at least another hour.

Keep in mind that my friend was a big guy and pretty tough. But this meant nothing against the mood swings of his five-foot-tall wife, who was relentless with her demands. To me, this was the equivalent of living in hell.

39

A good man doesn't stand a chance against this kind of woman. Traditionally, most guys believe you should never get physical no matter what the circumstances. This raises the question, what do you do if a woman jumps out of a dark alley welding a knife demanding your money? But I digress. Never put your hands on a woman is the motto. Unfortunately for you, if they know this is your mantra, they will undoubtedly take full advantage of the fact. You're expected to be patient and understand that they're just being emotional. After all, it's not like they can physically harm you. *Yeah right.* You're supposed to allow them to scream in your face, curse you out, challenge your manhood, and embarrass you in public.

But will she do the same for you when you are having a bad day? Will she have this same level of control and restraint when you are screaming and foaming at the mouth? Of course not. She would never stand for you, cursing her out and embarrassing her in public. "That's abuse," He exclaimed sarcastically. Besides, that's not what a "real man" does, right? Insert Shaming Language here. Ever notice the only time the "real man" conversation comes up is when it's time to excuse toxic female behavior?

Anger is an emotion, and sometimes, it's justified. But if she's allowed to be angry at the drop of a hat, but you're never allowed to be angry, that's not balanced. And without balance, you cannot have a healthy relationship.

She Is Selfish

She has hopes and dreams she wants to achieve. And she expects you to make those dreams happen. She wants a big house, an expensive luxury car, and enough jewelry to make the lucky charms leprechaun jealous. You're the man. You're supposed to make it happen. But what does she do? Does she work? Is she taking care of the home? Does she make sure the kids behave and do their schoolwork? Does she cook? Does she clean? Is her head game mean? No, because she's selfish. She wants you to take care of it all even though she's not worthy of any of it. And if you're unable to do it all, she'll have the nerve to tell you that you need a better job.

She wants a man who earns at least $100,000 a year but will stick with a job where she only earns $30,000 a year. She wants you to earn for her, pay her bills, and help her live a cushy life. But what is she giving you in return? Submission? Respect? Loyalty? Anything?

In addition, she will set boundaries that only apply to *you*.

Your boundaries don't matter at all. If you tell her she's crossed a boundary, she will find a way to flip it around and blame you. For example, you're not allowed to comment on a female friend's picture on social media, but she can comment on a male friend's picture.

She will justify it as "He's just a friend. The picture isn't inappropriate because he's not showing off his body parts." If you protest and call her out on her behavior, she will call you "controlling" and say you don't give her space to breathe. She might even accuse you of being insecure.

In the bedroom, she will want *you* to be the one pleasing her and will barely do anything to satisfy you. You have to "get her off," and you will hear about it for a few days if you can't. She will then blame it on you because you couldn't help her finish. You didn't even try.

You can't spend time with your friends or family, but you always seem to end up at her friends and family events. To this woman, it's all about her world and never about yours.

She Will Make You Feel Bad About Yourself

She will find a way to criticize you for everything you do. Whether it's the way you look or the things you do, you'll never be good enough. For example, if you gain weight, she will tell you you are no longer attractive and lazy. But if you tell her she's gaining weight, no matter how nicely you put it, she will start sobbing.

She will then proceed to tell you you're being a jerk and how her friends' boyfriends/husbands make them feel fabulous. Finally, she will list down everything her friends' boyfriends/husbands do for them and even bring up things her exes did for her that you can never measure up to.

She will never be happy with your effort because you will never live up to her standards. She will compare you to the men she's had a crush on. She will compare you to her exes, friends' boyfriends/husbands, her father, and even her brother.

She will want you to put in eighty to ninety percent of the effort in the relationship. So you need to look like a Greek god; you need to earn like Bill Gates and keep her happy all the time.

These expectations are unrealistic. She herself couldn't exceed or meet her own expectations if she was in your shoes. So you need to look out for these red flags. I always say, "If there are more red flags than China, you need to run in the opposite direction."

If you're dating a woman, I suggest you look out for these red flags before moving on to the next level. What is her attitude like at the start of the relationship? Refuse to get into a relationship until you *know* for sure that she doesn't make any of the points listed above.

44

This is why I suggest "vetting" before considering things like a long-term relationship or marriage. Once she knows she's got you where she wants you, it will be challenging to break free, especially after all the gaslighting, manipulations, and emotional abuse. You'll end up losing your identity and won't know which way is up. You'll be a broken man, too mentally weak to vote with your feet.

The last thing you want is a woman who will waste your time. High-caliber men need to be with women who know how to value them, treat them with respect, and take control of everything. She needs to understand that you're the man and only you lead the relationship.

Keep in mind that no woman is perfect. But what you want is a woman who's already dealt with her issues (if any) and has moved on. You don't want to become a babysitter or her therapist. You don't want the relationship to become a three-ring circus with you constantly jumping through hoops to satisfy her because there will be no satisfaction to be had, only more hoops. You're not there to heal her wounds. She is responsible for her experiences and traumas.

She shouldn't be dumping her emotional baggage on you. Paranoia and spontaneous anger are red flags. She should be more agreeable than disagreeable. She should know how to respect you. The last thing you want to deal with is a woman with a knack for drama. You want someone humble, kind, and down to earth.

If she is unpleasant to be around, aggressive, and challenges your authority, run the other way. It will not work out because she'll have a problem with everything and everyone in your life. She'll find problems where there are none. You'll lose your inner peace and your relationships because of her.

Many people will tell you to just accept her for who she is and be patient and gentle with her. But this is bullshit advice cultivated by a post-feminist society that excuses narcissistic female behavior. If she can't treat you with respect and dignity, then she is not the one for you. She needs to give you respect, space, and freedom. And she shouldn't be starting beef with other women in your life.

Considering all of this, now you know what to look out for when choosing a good woman. First, remember that a man needs to lead, and a woman needs to follow. Period.

Chapter 3:
The Agreement

"Men keep agreements when it is to the advantage of neither to break them."
-Solon

Women have always had a significant influence in the dating and mating marketplace. A man has always had to woo his lay and ensure he eliminates all competition. There is never a shortage of eligible suitors vying for her favor as they shower her with attention, affection, money, and validation. This endless pursuit gives women a multitude of options, a sad truth that ensures her position of power in the courting process. Most women won't hesitate to replace you as if you were a tradeable commodity. The nerve. But of course, she feels this way! Every guy out there pursuing women has a desire for the prettiest, sexiest trophy they can find. But be careful; everything that glitters ain't gold. Think of the sailors of the past who were led to their demise over the beauty and angelic song of the siren. All that sweet talk and all that kindness just goes out the window the moment you make it official, and she realizes that she has you right where she wants you. But nevertheless, she is the prize. Oh yes! This is what she believes. You are tired, stranded, and wandering in the desert, and she is an oasis you have been dying to discover.

When things don't work out, she has the confidence of knowing that plenty of guys are just waiting for you to "screw up," so they can have their shot at the title. Since there are plenty of suitors interested in her, she has a pool of talent to pick from—like American Idol. She can just sit behind a table judging all the guys performing like circus monkeys to be chosen. It's disgusting. She knows she can end up with someone more prosperous, handsome, and competent than you. And to add insult to injury, she'll never let you live it down; she will make sure you and everyone else know that she upgraded. She'll post that crap all over social media. Society—the feminist movement in particular—has built her up to think that regardless of what she may stand for and no matter how emotionally and mentally abusive she is, she can always do better. If not her family, her friends usually tell her that she is a *Queen and* deserves better. She could be an average chick, and you could do a thousand times better than her, but since she has been empowered to think she's the prize and to consider you just another option, she will always view you as her lessor.

Just like the praying mantis where the female murders the male right after mating with him successfully, she knows whatever she does, she will always get away with it. It is sad how society always sides with the damsel in distress. She will always get sympathy, attention, and even protection. In contrast, you will be called out for being a toxic and abusive jerk.

One must take a more professional and tactical approach to avoid all this. If you start seeing a woman, first, start viewing her as a potential employee you are looking to hire. This turns the tables (no pun intended). Now she's auditioning, and you're sitting behind the table in judgment of her. Let's be honest! What are modern-day relationships? Partnerships? I think they are arrangements in which both parties get to choose from the offset if they want to participate. Is that not what modern feminism wants? Equality and agency. Well, let's give them what they want! It's time for you to sack up and give her the truth without any fear of rejection. You must tell her the dating policy, just like a company educates their new hires on their latest and updated company policies, so they know what they are getting into. Most of you are in relationships, situationships, or arrangements already. The only problem is that most of you haven't even discussed terms, much less agreed upon anything.

Now, don't be a coward and withhold anything that might be a turn-off or manipulate her by sugarcoating the truth. She has already told you that she prefers honesty. Give it to her raw! The cold, hard truth! Explain to her exactly what she's getting into. Treat her like an equal, give her agency, and allow her to choose if she wants to be a part of your program. Allow her to be the big girl she demands the world to see her as.

Lay down the rules. Let her know the things you want and like, but most of all, the things you will not accept. Set your boundaries. Yes! If she can have specific boundaries, you can too. Tell her how it's going to be. Let her know that if she breaks your rules, it will be the end of the relationship. Tell her what her role will be when she becomes your lady. No matter how big or how small. If you don't want her hanging out in the living room while you and your friends are watching the game, tell her that. It's only fair because she expects you not to be all up in her face when she's chatting with her female friends; she should respect you and not parade herself around your friends like some desperate housewife looking for male attention. Giving her your rules upfront can never be viewed as a form of control because she has the choice to accept or decline, just like a job offer. If she accepts the job knowing what it entails, that is her choice. From the start, she knows what she's signing up for.

Let's say, hypothetically, that you are not about that party life. Tell her! Tell her you are a homebody, and you don't like wasting time drinking at a club, paying double and even triple for watered-down drinks. You value your time and money, and you like spending time at home watching a game or just being a lazy bum. Now she can decide if she wants to stay with someone who doesn't like to party, or she can kick rocks and go find a guy who likes to get wild for the night. If she can have a *'Take it or leave it'* attitude, you can too! If she still chooses to stay, then she made the decision on her own, knowing the whole truth. Tell her that respect is a 2-way street; if she wants your respect, she will have to earn it and give it in return. Ensure that she understands that (to a man) there is nothing more important than respect in this world.

If you're frugal, tell her you don't go on shopping sprees, spending money like it's going out of style. If you're extravagant and love to spend lavishly, tell her that you spend your money how you want to, and at no point will she be dictating how you manage your finances. You get the point. It's all about what you want and how you want to roll. Stop me if you've heard this one. One guy tells his buddy that his wife wanted a new pet, but he didn't. His buddy asked him what they decided. He said we compromised and got a new pet. Don't be that guy. Don't be a pussy.

Again, you are the employer, and she is looking for a job. She wanted the job, and she asked for the interview. Don't be a coward. Be straight up and honest—even cold if the situation demands. You are a multinational company with a 401k, a pleasant working environment, and a ton of benefits. She should put in her work and prove her worth! She needs to show you that she can be trusted with the position she is applying for. Either she meets your requirements, or you will go with another more qualified applicant.

In the end, fellas, it's better to find out upfront whether the chick is the right fit for you or not. Being completely honest about what you want and don't want is the fastest way. As much as women claim to love honesty, it's just not true. Most women hate an uncomfortable truth. They prefer that things are left unsaid. Why? For plausible deniability. You can't possibly hold them accountable for something they don't know. And trust me, they know. They just pretend they don't to escape agency and responsibility for their actions. Therefore, the job analogy is perfect. Women follow the workplace rules with no problem. Why? Because they're told upfront what their responsibilities are. This way, later, they can't pretend they didn't know when to fail to do their job. Laying everything out upfront will deter any woman who is not up to the task, just like an interview for an extremely demanding job. But this is a good thing. It weeds out all the undesirables.

Remember to treat your initial interaction with her like an employer interviewing your future potential employee. There is no harm in having an honest and open conversation when both parties are sane, intellectual adults with no emotional investment and nothing to lose. Make her understand that she cannot have her cake and eat, too. She must meet your requirements to even be considered. She may have power in the dating and mating world, but you hold the keys to the relationship. And that's where the security, money, and benefits are, just like a job.

And if she doesn't like what you say or can't accept your requirements, you both can just call it off before you get attached and go your separate ways. But I guarantee you that only good women will make it to a second interview.

Chapter 4:
Do Not Date Single Mothers

"Single mother is an oxymoron. The guy who dates her is just a moron."

-The Angryman

No one in life ever plans to have a failed relationship. Nobody approaches a potential mate, thinking to themselves, "I'm pretty sure this interaction will end in disaster." Every relationship starts from a pure place of honesty (or at least we hope it does). It's very simple. You spot someone you find attractive, get your nerves up, and risk rejection to make some sort of connection. Only time will tell if it's a lasting connection. And therein lies the problem. It really is a numbers game when you think about it. However, life is too short to spend going from one bad relationship to the next just trying to figure out your best option. I'm not saying you should marry your high school sweetheart or dive into the dating scene searching for that elusive unicorn. Let's be serious. That sort of thing doesn't exist. But what I am telling you is before starting any relationship, you need to have a very discerning eye. And part of that means knowing the time-saving technique of identifying who to disqualify from the offset.

So, who can we immediately disqualify from our dating options? Considering the title of the chapter, I'm pretty sure you already know the answer. But what you don't know is the why. Why is dating a single mother such a bad thing to do?

Well, let me start with a disclaimer. I'm not saying single mothers are horrible people. I'm not saying they're not deserving of relationships or even love. I'm pretty sure there are some single mothers out there who are wonderful. The only problem is that they're the exception and not the rule—a rare exception, like that unicorn we previously mentioned. And please don't get into your feelings. Even if you were raised by a single mother, you are going to have to face reality. You have to stop looking at the single mother issue as a son trying to save his mother and start looking at it the right way—as a man trying to spare his potential child(ren) the dysfunction you had to endure.

No. For a single, childless man who's serious about finding a viable, well-rounded, responsible, intelligent, submissive, cooperative woman with whom he can build a bond, a single mother is never a good option.

Let's start with the most obvious reasons.

First Choice: If she's a single mother, there's a strong possibility that you're not, nor will you ever be, her first choice. I believe this because of two things: novelty and Oxytocin. Novelty is when humans experience something for the first time. Oxytocin, also known as the love drug, is a hormone and neurotransmitter involved in childbirth and breastfeeding. It's also associated with empathy, trust, sexual activity, and relationship building. I believe these two things combined are responsible for imprinting—the bond between a man and woman (we will go into more detail about bonding later). A woman's first sexual partner, especially the first man to impregnate her, is hard to compete with. Or, as Sade put it, "It's never as good as the first time."

Past Performance: The fact that she is a single mother is 100% proof that she failed at relationships. And past performance is an indicator of future performance. We don't know if it was her fault or not, but that's irrelevant. What we do know is that two people decided to create a life. One of the most important decisions you'll ever make. And for some reason, that all-important decision wasn't strong enough to keep them together, not to mention the lack of desire to ensure the best options for said life. This speaks directly to a lack of priorities and poor decision-making skills. I am not saying that mistakes don't happen. I'm not even saying it's impossible for a single mother to have a successful relationship. But I can say that dating a single mother comes with a host of unexpected problems that I wouldn't wish on my worst enemy. Take it from someone who knows.

Immaturity: Most people today won't agree, but getting pregnant outside of a marriage is a sign of immaturity and lack of planning. The sad part is that, in most cases, this isn't a mistake. Today, women get pregnant for numerous reasons. The least of which include having a family and raising a productive member of society. Keep in mind that this doesn't necessarily apply to divorced or widowed women. These types can be an exception depending on the circumstances. As a rule of thumb, anytime a woman gets pregnant outside the security of marriage, you have to question the motives. The reason is that women have over twenty-five different types of birth control available to them. Even if they have the child, they can give it up for adoption or just leave it on the steps of a fire station. I'm serious. We live in a world where men go to jail for not supporting a child, but women can abandon babies with no consequences. The reality is this. No woman today has a child unless she wants to have a child. Doing it outside of marriage definitely raises an eyebrow. In most cases, her being immature is the least of the problems.

Bonding: When two people start and maintain a lasting, successful relationship, they develop a strong bond that's difficult to break. In a normal relationship, the primary bond is the husband/wife bond. Later comes the secondary parent/child bond, which is shared between the two parents and the child(ren). When a woman becomes a single mother, there is no primary husband/wife bond. There isn't even a secondary parent/child bond. There is only the mother/child bond. And that bond is not only primary but exclusive. Any man trying to date a single mother will never be able to develop the husband/wife bond because the mother/child bond will always override everything else. One could even argue that only a selfish man would expect a mother to choose him over her child. And I agree. This is something that cannot be ignored. If you want to develop a strong relationship bond with your mate, it has to be pre- or post-child. This means she hasn't had a child yet, or for you older guys, the children are grown and out of the house. And we haven't even mentioned your interaction with a child that's not yours. A complicated issue that, I assure you, no man is prepared for. This is why the normal relationship process is best. The child has to view the two of you in the same light. And the two of you have to view the child in the same light. To the child, both of you are the parents. And to the two of you, this is your child. This is virtually impossible in a single-mother situation. From all aspects, you will always be on the outside looking in. This issue can be detrimental to your mental health. Being in a relationship in which you feel excluded can cause loneliness, isolation, anxiety, and depression. And any complaints you raise will make you seem childish and selfish. She may even accuse you of being jealous of her child. It's simply not worth it.

Poly-Nogamy: (Poly-Nogamy is not technically a word, but it's a term I invented, which is a combination of polygamy and monogamy, which is what most people are engaged in today.) When you get into a relationship with a single mother, that doesn't end her relationship with the father of her child. The three of you are now locked into a threesome of bullshit. They may or may not be having sex, but they are inseparably tied to one another because of this child. For some of the lucky ones, the father is a deadbeat who's completely out of the picture. Lucky for you, but not for her or the child. His absence presents problems as well. Or, in other unfortunate circumstances, the father is diseased. Either way, the child not being yours presents a whole host of problems. But let's get back to the normal scenario. When the father is in the picture, this will always present a problem. Prior to you meeting her, he did not care about the situation. But now that you are in the picture, he wants to be the best dad that ever lived. God forbid anyone should replace him. Or worse. He wants to win her love back. These situations always ignite the male competition gene. What happens if the child is disrespectful to you? Surely, you cannot discipline the child. After all, he's not yours. To him, you are just some strange man his mom is dating. And you cannot keep running to the mother every time the child does something wrong. It looks weak. Neither the mother nor the child will respect you. But at the same time, you cannot take it upon yourself to discipline the child. This will cause a problem with the biological father. Maybe even the mother. A mother's protective instincts will always kick in when the child is in distress. This makes it impossible for a stepfather to discipline a stepchild. It does not matter how right you are. Biology supersedes the progressive social conditions of today. Trust me. It is a no-win situation. Besides, it is impossible to lead a woman who has another man in her ear.

Legacy: Here's the part that's too complicated even to comprehend. Let's say you date a single mother. And let's say you marry her and have children. Now you have a splintered family. How about if your wife's child's father has another kid with another woman? Now, your child is related to your stepchild but not related to your stepchild's sibling. See how complicated this is becoming. Part of legacy is being able to trace back your lineage. How could you possibly do that if your grandfather had children with a woman who had children by three other men? And those men had children with other women. It would get to the point where people wouldn't even know if they're related to one another. And please forgive me. This explanation sounds like gibberish, but only because it's difficult to make sense of this type of dysfunction. If merely explaining it is complicated and confusing, imagine the damage it's causing to the social fabric of our society.

I'm not saying that you can't have similar problems with other types of relationships. Dating a woman who doesn't have any child will not guarantee you an awesome relationship. However, on the flip side, the prospect of a child will always be a huge factor in any relationship. The fact that people take this so lightly in this day and age speaks volumes. In the not-too-distant past, this behavior was frowned upon. Today, it's being celebrated as some sort of honor, even though all the data we have on this subject proves that children raised in single-parent homes do not fair well as children in two-parent homes. Yet, we continue to promote and reward this behavior. Using the evidence going back to the sixties, one could argue that the single mother led to the destruction of the nuclear family.

We could draw quite a few conclusions that illustrate the major problems with our society today; however, that is not the purpose of this book. The purpose of this book is to give you gentlemen the best outcome possible. The average guy might not have a problem with dating a single mother. And many of the issues we've raised here may be of no concern to those individuals. However, we are not trying to create average situations. In today's climate of anti-male, anti-family, anti-patriarch rhetoric, we're trying to do the extraordinary. Part of that means abstaining from the pitfalls of the average Joe. Not dating single mothers should be a universal rule for all single, childless men. There are exceptions to the rule, but wouldn't you rather be on the safe side instead of trying to find that one exception that justifies your choice?

Think about it like this. Let's say you want to purchase a home. You begin your house hunt and find a home that looks awesome on the outside. We're talking serious curb appeal. You even start thinking about how jealous your friends will be when they see it. Then you go inside, and guess what? You hate the inside. The entire inside of the house would have to be renovated. The only problem is you'd have to buy the house before you could even begin calculating the cost, time, and effort to make the changes. This will require one hell of a commitment. Now you have a choice. Do you buy the house because of its curb appeal, or do you keep looking? The logical option is to keep looking and get what you want. Anything less would mean you are settling. Anyone will tell you buying a house that you have to renovate just because you dislike the ascetics is not the best option. Depending on the cost, you may end up purchasing the house twice. And there's no guarantee you'll be able to do all the renovations. In some cases, the headache of renovating the house is so overwhelming that you just want to get rid of it. It's that shining moment when you realize you took on more than you can handle.

Well, many of you have this same problem when it comes to women. You meet a gorgeous woman. She has big breasts, a pretty face, a big booty, and a slim waist. You haven't even got the number yet, and you already imagine how your friends will react to your future goddess. But upon further inspection, you find out she has other issues. Either she's a horrible person inside, or she has a child from a previous relationship. And just like that house with the awesome curb appeal, you think you can renovate. Her looks are just too good to pass on. And before you know it, you find yourself locked into a mortgage(I mean relationship), desperately trying to make sense of the situation. Ultimately, you always end up never finishing those renovations and getting rid of the failed project(relationship) altogether. It would have been better to keep searching. Yes, the search is long and difficult, but definitely worth it if you get what you want. It's always better to find the exact house you want. One that looks good, with no surprises and very few, if any, problems. If possible, you can even build it from the ground up. But the one thing you can take away from this chapter is this: Never buy someone else's problems.

Chapter 5: Standard #2: The Position of Power

"A woman can never elevate a Man to his highest level. If I'm King, I can make any woman Queen, but the Queen can't make any Man the King. I'm better than you."

-Patrice O'Neal

Whether you're an old-ass baby boomer or a young emotional millennial, whether you're a hardheaded Gen Xer or a bright-eyed Gen Z, one thing is certain: you are a man. And man has been blessed with the mantle of leadership. By virtue of being born a man, it is your birthright to rule. Does this mean you should behave like a tyrant and constantly boast about your power? No, not at all! Rather, you should revel in the fact that history has proven that your role in society as individuals or groups justifies your power and position.

The world has become a strange place where society is socialized to take that sense of power and strength away from men, primarily under the banner of feminism. Everything that is traditionally male is viewed as toxic or evil due to a few rotten apples. Competition, aggression, and dominance, just to name a few, are discouraged among young boys. The attitudes and ideological views that created our society and propelled us to the top of the food chain are now viewed as wrong. Ultimately, the males in upcoming generations will face a major identity crisis. Why should men have to justify our nature simply because evil men do evil deeds? Do men start wars? Yes. But how many times has a woman been the cause of that war? How many times has a woman been the source and cause of conflict between powerful men? Do we now boycott female nature? Do we march in the streets with picket signs proclaiming women to be the source of all evil? Of course not. But what we can do is reject the premise that being unapologetically male is toxic.

The only way this can be done is to reject the false ideology of feminism completely. You must drive it from your home like a priest casts out demons. If you truly desire to be the King of your castle, feminism can have no place in your home or your life. Moreover, never date a woman claiming to be or behaving like a feminist. This should go without saying, but don't waste your time. Feminism should be viewed as a profane word. This must be understood before you can begin to grasp the concept of the position of power. So, how does one gain the coveted position of power? Throughout time, men have utilized various methods to solidify their power. In our primitive past, we've used brute force and even violence, two things that are frowned upon in today's civilized world. Today, men use their words, charm and finesse. Instead of trying to possess the woman physically, we aim to possess her mentally. Either way, regardless of your skills or methods, one thing is certain: all powerful men have money.

Make no mistake: men with money aren't always powerful; powerful men always have money. And money is how you maintain your position of power. I am a firm believer that without money to solidify your position, it's going to be very difficult to live a life of respect, honor, and dignity. The reason is that women cannot respect a man who doesn't have resources. And there's nothing in this world more important than respect. Not even love. But remember, as we stated before, men with money aren't always powerful. Money alone will not guarantee you the position of power. There are plenty of men who shower women with money, yet they still get played. Money is simply the foundation upon which you build your throne. The more money, the stronger the foundation. It is from that point that you begin to build your program.

But why is money so important? It's simple. It's not that money in and of itself is so important. It's what the money represents. For men, money should represent power and nothing else. Never forget that. For women, money represents food, shelter, comfort, security, etc. Ask any woman why she wants a man with money, and you'll get a laundry list of needs, wants, and desires. Regardless of their lengthy wish list, women only want one thing from men: women want men to achieve for them. And that's not to say that women aren't capable. Women can achieve plenty. But why put in the work to achieve something if someone else is willing to achieve it for you? This is the mantra of women throughout the ages, even if they aren't willing to admit it. Why do for yourself what someone else can do for you? And plenty of money certainly makes this possible. The trick is making her earn it.

The problem with most of you men is you treat the woman like the prize. The moment she gets with you, you think you're supposed to shower her with money and gifts. Basically, rewarding her for being with you. Her mere presence is worth your money? This is insanity. What reward did she give you for being with her? Ask her this question, and I guarantee she'll say she is the reward. But this is no fair exchange. You get her and nothing else, but she gets you and your money. That's robbery. And in that scenario, you have no power. You gave it all away on day one. You have absolutely nothing to bargain with. Unacceptable. Let's reevaluate the situation. In fact, let's think of it like you're playing poker. After all, relationships are a gamble. In most cases, the man approaches the woman first, which means he's the first to ante up.

This means you present yourself as the initial bet to see what cards you're dealt. Now, it's on the woman to ante up and match your initial bet by presenting herself if she wants to play the game. Now she gets her cards. So, from the offset, the two of you have an equal stake in the dating/mating/relationship game. Now, let's say you like the cards you have and are ready to play. In other words, you like the situation. You might choose to raise the bet by adding money to the relationship. You can do this by taking her out or buying her something nice. But keep in mind, once you do this, it is now on her to match or raise your bet. What can she bet? She could bet submission, respect, or whatever. It depends on what you think is equal to your last bet. Most of you never get this far. The reason is that she never offers anything beyond the initial bet, but you keep raising the pot. She doesn't even fold. She just continues to sit at the table, which is against the rules. But you don't care. You're just happy she's at the table. Pretty soon, the only thing on the table is you and all your money. At least until you finally fold, and she walks off with all of your money, not to mention your pride.

No. The way to win the game is to make her play by your rules instead of making up her own. If you raise the pot, she needs to match you; otherwise, the game stops. If she can't match or raise, she has to fold. If she has nothing of value to offer, she shouldn't be sitting at the table in the first place. It's all about value. She must match your value. The trick is to raise it right after she matches. Because you have the most value in the situation, you're always raising the pot. And she's always attempting to match the pot. This creates an endless loop of her chasing you instead of you chasing her. This may seem wrong, but it's not. Women love to look up to a man as opposed to looking down on him. Every woman wants a winner. The day that she has more value is the day that she buys the pot and walks off with everything. This is when hypergamy works against you. When you're constantly raising the pot, hypergamy works for you.

Constantly having more value helps to maintain your position of power. For this purpose, one should always focus on earning more money than his woman. This is not to say that money is the only thing of value. We just illustrated that women could offer things of value that aren't monetary because men value the intangibles just as much as the tangibles. Sometimes more. However, we know that most things women value can be purchased with money. It's a bitter fact, but the person in the relationship with the most money indeed has the most power. But what men and women do with that power is drastically different. When the man has the money, the woman is at his feet; when the woman has the money, the man is on the street. A bit chauvinistic, but true. Men have no problem taking care of women, but women have no desire to take care of men. There once was a time when men could achieve this with nothing more than their hunting and building abilities. Those days are gone. Today, all the things we could hunt, kill, make, and build, we must buy. We must realize that we live in a materialistic world, and all the comforts of life require money.

Whether you like it or not, the measure of a man today is based on the money he can generate.

Aside from earning more money, another key to the position of power is ensuring that you're paying 100% of the household bills whether she lives with you or not. Keep in mind that if she does live with you, this does not include her personal bills like cell phone expenses, etc. Your responsibility is to pay everything you would pay if she weren't living there. Apart from bills, all the important assets should be in your name. The key to this is making sure that she understands that if she leaves tomorrow, your situation won't skip a beat. Many women get a kick out of knowing that you need them financially and will often use that fact to leverage power. Never a good situation to be in.

Older cats used to say, "No romance without finance." And rightfully so. This may seem like an unfair double standard, but it's just reality. Any woman worth her salt will always want a financially stable man. Think about it in terms of value. What is it that you value about a woman?

Are you willing to be with a woman who doesn't have that thing that you value? Of course not. Unless you're a simp. Therefore, you cannot expect women to want broke men. Women value resources. They always have, and they always will. It's hardwired into their DNA. Changing that part of female nature would be like trying to transform lead into gold. It's impossible. But why are women designed that way? It's simple. Children. Women have a biological urge to secure resources for themselves and their potential offspring. Women highly desire men who can provide provision, procreation, and protection.

Some of you may disagree with my assessments. You may even believe I'm crazy for suggesting you pay 100% of the bills. I understand your reluctance. Women of today work just as much as men. They even claim independence. And the last thing you want is to feel like you're being used. Why should she be able to live without the burden of household bills? After all, she is an adult. Now, we arrive at the good old 50/50 arrangement—the equal partnership. Anyone who suggests or believes that a 50/50 partnership with your woman will work either hasn't been in a relationship yet or has found that magical unicorn we discussed earlier. The reason why it doesn't work is simple. 50/50 makes you more like partners. But you're not in a partnership; you're in a relationship. The difference is subtle but very important. This partnership idea is just a more feminist subversion. Think about this. When you have a roommate, you have a 50/50 arrangement. This dynamic works with a roommate because the two of you have your own possessions and your own space. And more importantly, you're not fucking each other. There's no expectation to share everything. In other words, you have well-established boundaries. You both have your own room. You both have your own bed. The only thing you really share is the common areas of the apartment/house. In a relationship, you share everything. It's almost viewed as an insult if you don't. What's mine is yours, and what's yours is mine—until it's not.

You both have 50% ownership, which leads to the inevitable fight over who controls what you own. When you have 100% ownership over the household and the bills, this fight never occurs. But if a woman owns just 10% of anything, she behaves as if she owns it all. With women, if she's in for a penny, she's in for a pound, and if you give them an inch, they will most certainly take a mile. What I've found in my experience is when you pay the cost to be the boss, women rarely try to pull rank. However, let them contribute one dollar to the cause and they want to run the entire show. Plus, 50/50 is too close to a controlling interest. You guys know how corporate partnerships work. In a 50/50 partnership, all your partner needs is 1% more to make it 51/49 in their favor. Now, your partner has just become your boss. This always happens with men in 50/50 relationships. And most of them don't even know how it happened. I'll tell you how it happened. You were equal right up until you had children. In a 50/50 relationship, children are a liability for men and an asset to women. Why is this? Because if the woman gets tired of your 50% input, she can use the children to get government assistance to replace your 50% contribution, therefore usurping your half of the power. When you pay 100%, you become an asset to both your woman and children because the government might provide enough to replace 50%, but I guarantee they won't replace 100%.

Remember this: you can't maintain the position if your woman has the same position. At that point, she can easily tip the scale in her favor or just outright replace you. Why listen to you when she has just as much invested? Why submit when she can leverage her position? You've set the bar too low. If you're at 100%, she can't tip the scale. That mountain is too high to climb. Those resources are too hard to replace. Take it from someone who's been in both situations. Having a woman pay half the bills is a weight off your shoulders, and you can definitely benefit from the situation monetarily. However, I guarantee you that the bullshit you will endure due to her having "equal" power will far outweigh any benefit you think you might enjoy. It's not worth it.

Chapter 6: Standard # 3: Non-State Sanctioned Marriage

"Those who talk most about the blessings of marriage and the constancy of its vows are the very people who declare that if the chain were broken and the prisoners left free to choose, the whole social fabric would fly asunder. You cannot have the argument both ways. If the prisoner is happy, why lock him in? If he is not, why pretend he is? "

-George Bernard Shaw, Man and Superman

Women have always made the claim that they desire good men. But what is a good man? How do women define a good man? Is a good man a man with money? If that's the case, how ridiculous is it that a woman will find a man with plenty of money, but the moment he does one little thing wrong, she's ready to leave him? Regardless, money is always part of the equation. Does this mean your ability to be a good mate is based simply on financial stability? Do we just toss other aspects of masculinity in the trash? What about the other qualities, such as kindness, loyalty, leadership, etc.? Does any of that hold any value, or is it just his financial stability?

It seems today that all women are interested in is what you can do for them monetarily. This is why standard #2 is so effective. It gives you a powerful tool to secure your position of power, but only if structured the right way. Women who find themselves in relationships with financially stable men are always pushing to get married because they know this arrangement will secure their present and future. Simply being in a relationship is never enough. Albeit, making a verbal commitment and sliding a ring on each other's finger should be enough. Oh no. For this to be real, we need to "put it on paper." We need a legally binding contract. But why?

Why is the marriage license such an important part of this equation? It's simple. Without the contract, you can't be forced to provide financial support for a woman you no longer want to be with. Don't get me wrong, the marriage contract was important and served its purpose in the days of old. But it has yet to be updated. In this day of equality and women's proclamations of strength and independence, the marriage contract still treats women as if they are helpless children who do not have the ability to earn sufficient wages. Supposedly, in our male-dominated world, women need a failsafe that puts the onus on their future ex-husband to continue to provide for them should the marriage fail. Not only is this premise ridiculous for today's world, but it's dangerous. This concept gives any woman at any given time the right to divorce any man for any reason. It's called no-fault divorce. This brings me to the million-dollar question.

Why is the woman's financial security more important than the man's? If we understand the concept of women wanting to be protected through the concept of financial security, why can't we understand the same for men? Is his protection any less important than hers? If women can opt into getting married for security, then why can't men opt out of marriage for the same reason? This is called "The Irresistible Force Paradox." This is when an unstoppable force crashes into an immovable object. Marriage has become the ultimate contradiction—a zero-sum game.

The legal system does not have a single law that protects a man's finances from divorce. In fact, it seems today that divorce court is designed strictly to extract money from unsuspecting men. As if men have some preordained obligation to take care of every woman he has ever been in a relationship with for the rest of their lives. Don't get me wrong, I believe a man should take care of his family, but just because a man's wife decides to end the relationship (for whatever reason) doesn't mean he should continue to be financially obligated to her. To be honest, he shouldn't be obligated in the first place. It should be a choice, his choice. And just as easily as he chose to take care of her, he can also choose to decline. His only obligation should be to his children, if any. And even that financial obligation shouldn't be determined by the state.

What's truly unfortunate about these situations is that no one ever factors into man's humanity. In other words, where is the sympathy? Marriage, divorce, and even child support are always discussed in a very cold way. Men are treated like beasts of burden, only here for the utilitarian purpose of providing monetary support for ungrateful women and children. How unfair is it that a man should have to face not only financial ruin but heartbreak and the pain of parental alienation as well? Whether the man is rich or poor, if his wife chooses to leave him, he will surely pay a hefty price. With that in mind, take this next bit of advice with a grain of salt and proceed cautiously. I'm not against marriage, but I'm not a fool either.

Many of you have chosen to abstain from marriage, whether traditional or not. And I don't blame you. Marriage today is a bad contract. But I do realize that some of you want to be married. In fact, most of you would be married right now if it wasn't for a no-fault divorce. This tells me that you don't mind the marriage part. It's the "getting taken for all your money" part that you're trying to avoid. So, for those of you who still believe in the institution of marriage and want to give it a try, I'm going to do my best to give you the most viable options that will hopefully reduce the risk of financial ruin.

The first thing you need to understand is that signing a marriage license exposes you to financial liability. Rather than getting bound in a marriage where a legal marriage license is issued, one can go for a wedding ceremony with no marriage license, which excludes the state. This is what I refer to as a non-state-sanctioned marriage. You can have all the bells and whistles of a normal wedding. You can even exchange rings. But no official marriage license. Most women won't like this option for various reasons, mainly because there are certain rights and protections that a wife enjoys due to the state recognizing the marriage. However, this can easily be fixed with other documents. The couple can opt for a domestic partnership and cohabitation agreement. Each of these options offers a few benefits, like traditional marriage, and has pros and cons but eliminates her ability to fleece you for all your hard-earned money in divorce court. Other than that, the couple can go for a private marriage contract. It may vary from state to state, but the point is to have a private contract between two people that does not include the state.

On a side note, be sure to check the laws in your state concerning marriage and cohabitation. Not every state is the same. Some jurisdictions can hold you liable for simply cohabitating with a woman for an extended period. You could be on the hook financially just for living with a chick, not necessarily married. It's called palimony, which is defined as the division of financial assets and real property on the termination of a personal live-in relationship wherein the parties are not legally married. Cohabitate with a woman and her children, and you can find yourself not only paying her palimony, but you might even end up paying child support for children that are not yours. So make sure you know the laws of your state before you make any type of long-term relationship decision. In some cases, even cohabitation has the same legal ramifications as an official marriage.

So, with that being said, I feel like some of you are still planning on getting married officially, which I DO NOT ADVISE. However, if you cannot avoid an official marriage with a marriage license with the state, here's the process and course of action I suggest you take.

1. The Courting Period: Date multiple women for a one to three-year period. Ensure that the women know upfront that you're merely playing the field and have no desire to commit to anyone anytime soon. Ensure they know you're cool with them dating other guys. This will be important later. And this should go without saying, but make sure you wrap it up. NO RAW SEX, EVER. And do not cohabitate with this woman. You keep your place, and she keeps hers. Remember the employer analogy from earlier in the book. You're like a corporate headhunter looking for talent. You want to find the best candidate for the job. And you certainly can't get angry if your potential employee is entertaining other offers. Towards the end of the third year, it will become clear who the best choice is. She will be the one who:

A. Stuck around for three years

B. Wasn't jealous about you dating other chicks

C. Decided to stop dating other guys because she only wanted you

2. Committed Relationship: Now, you can stop dating other chicks and start a serious relationship. She's proven herself to a degree. She stuck around for a while, respected your boundaries, didn't get jealous, and made you her first choice. Consider this an evaluation period. The two of you can spend more time together. STILL, WRAP IT UP AND DO NOT COHABITATE. It's cool to spend the night at each other's place, but don't give up your space just yet. Now is the time to find out what she's really about. Whether she has any really bad habits or horrible family members, remember, if you marry a chick, you connect yourself to her family, too. This process should take no less than three years but no more than five. By year five, you should know for sure whether or not you want to be engaged to this woman.

3. Engagement: Now, we move to the next level. This is what I like to call the probationary period. This is when the rubber meets the road. This is when you find out if you want to spend the rest of your life with this woman. Now, you can cohabitate. This is when we find out if she can actually be your wife. Does she cater to you? Is she supportive? Does she still respect your boundaries now that she's in your space? Is she still submissive, or has she gotten comfortable? Does she still respect you, or has the security of a wedding ring exposed her true intentions? This period is when you will find out all. Like the previous, this should be no less than three years, no more than five.

4. Marriage: Never marry anyone you haven't known and engaged with for at least ten years. Seems pretty long, but better safe than sorry. Also, before you get married, you can set up an ironclad prenuptial agreement. I am sure you all know what a prenup is, but for those who don't, it's a contract mutually agreed upon by the two people planning to get married. This contract can potentially state each one's responsibilities and property rights for

as long as the marriage prevails. It determines who gets what should the marriage end. However, keep in mind that not all prenups are honored. Judges have been known to disregard prenups in their rulings, especially if children are involved.

Overall, my suggestion is non-state-sanctioned marriage in a jurisdiction that doesn't recognize common law marriage or palimony. Either that or go through the long process of vetting the woman properly in order to avoid any surprises. And let's face it, even then, you may be in for a shock. One thing I know for certain: in life, there are no guarantees. Just know that either way you cut it, marriage is a risk. And with all risks, you enter into them at your own peril. With marriage today, there is no ideal situation. All we can do is preemptively plan for any situation like a master tactician. Or you can just avoid it together. The choice is yours.

Chapter 7: Standard # 4: Reward/Punishment System

"A person who has been punished is not thereby simply less inclined to behave in a given way; at best, he learns how to avoid punishment."

-B.F. Skinner

The father of Operant Conditioning, B.F. Skinner, experimented to see whether or not a living body responds to the reward/punishment phenomenon or not. The reward was deemed as positive reinforcement, and on the other hand, the punishment was deemed as negative reinforcement. Skinner analyzed animal behavior by observing when an animal performed the desired action and was rewarded for it through the experiment. That experiment helped him determine how long it took the animal to learn to achieve a specific behavior.

There is a reason this experiment is still quoted and discussed to this day. Humans are highly triggered by reward and punishment. Therefore, they mold their behavior according to the results that they will receive.

Society is constantly reinforcing the false concept that women are the only innocent victims on the face of the earth. By doing this, they create the narrative that anything a woman does is never wrong. In fact, today, women are immensely praised for doing wrong. In this day and age, an unruly, disrespectful, wild woman is considered strong and independent. Thus, the praise is interpreted as a reward, encouraging more behavior. On the other hand, man is portrayed as a cruel beast whose patriarchal structure has only served as a repressive dictatorial system hell-bent on oppressing women. Which means men are being punished for being patriarchal. This poses a problem considering the fact that it was that very system of patriarchy that has allowed us to rise to the top of the food chain and cultivate and maintain a civilized society. While it is true that no system has ever been perfect, everything has its tradeoffs. I would argue that the benefits of patriarchy far outweigh its shortcomings.

Even the women know this to be true. If not, they wouldn't constantly complain about the lack of "real men" available today. It is not uncommon to hear women complaining and turning for the men of yesteryear while simultaneously encouraging a culture that shuns any man who dares to display the so-called "toxic" behavior of our forefathers. In modern society, we constantly pretend that we can achieve equality between the sexes. This is impossible. Our differences prohibit this. However, through the attempt at achieving this goal, we seem to have amplified the perception of the worst qualities of both genders— woman as the weak, innocent victim and man as the cruel beast.

The only problem is due to the nature of things, and one group benefits immensely from this amplifying of our worst qualities. Would you like to guess who?

Of course, it would be the women. Women's victimhood being amplified only serves to help their agenda. And amplifying the narrative that men are cruel beasts also serves to help women's agenda. See how that works? Carrying the title of "cruel beast" guarantees that, as a man, you will receive less empathy and zero to no understanding. Today's world is not only tolerant of anti-male misandry, but it also seems to celebrate it. And why not? Who wouldn't celebrate the taming of a cruel beast? Or the slaying of one? This is why a man must fortify his mind and learn what it truly means to be respected despite the narrative of this man-hating world we live in. I've often said, "You must train people in the fashion in which you want to be treated." In other words, train those around you to treat you with dignity and respect— especially your woman.

Once you've cultivated your self-respect, you must demand that others respect you as much as you do because you are not a beast to be tamed, slain, or enslaved. You are a man to be respected. You earned that. You deserve that despite the fact that society is trying to punish you for being a man. Without respect, you will not have cooperation and compliance. This puts your kingdom in disarray. And what king can enjoy peace of mind with his kingdom in turmoil?

Having self-respect and maintaining your integrity is vital. The man was not created to be a puppet, dancing on a string for women's amusement. Traditionally, the man is dominant, and the woman is submissive. However, today, these roles have been reversed. This is justified by the idea that men are cruel beasts who rule not for the purpose of order but only to oppress women. This can't be further from the truth. Men rule with logic and order. Women attempt to rule through manipulation and chaos. Women today believe that they should be the household authority figure at the very least. At most, they want to be the world authority figure. As a man, you must correct this error and set things back on the correct course. But first, you must understand how women condition men.

If you observe the average household, women become more dominant with time. How do they do this? It's simple. It involves a clever version of the aforementioned reward/punishment system. Or social conditioning. But with a few subtle tweaks. First, it starts with a relentless gaslighting campaign. They begin by finding little things to blame you for on a daily basis. This keeps you in a constant state of being wrong, which gives her endless opportunities to correct you as if you were a child. Think about it. If you're constantly wrong, by comparison, this makes her constantly right. Some examples of this include fussing with you about leaving your clothes lying on the floor or not putting the toilet seat down. It always starts with small, arbitrary things that aren't worth arguing about. Women understand that most men would rather avoid the argument altogether. This is the "happy wife, happy life" ideology. Picking up the clothes or putting the toilet seat down is easier than arguing daily. Or is it? This is how you lose your power. This is how you're trained to be a submissive man. Manipulative women slowly and methodically utilize this method to establish themselves as the authority figure of the household. The old folks used to call this "hen pecking." The reason why it works is that, logically, men would rather have peace in their homes as opposed to chaos. Small arguments become larger arguments, and soon, it becomes too stressful to even cohabitate with the woman. Most men today would rather fold. Some men are even socialized to believe that arguing with a woman is weak and not manly. And therein lies the genius. The strategy is based on our nature or, at the very least, our social conditioning based on society's standard of what a man is supposed to be. Either way, men are naturally benevolent towards women—especially women in our personal lives. And women take full advantage of this.

The sad part is that even though this is definitely an example of conditioning like B.F. Skinner speaks of it, it's not really a reward/punishment system because there's never really a reward. It's a corrupted version of conditioning. Think about it. The woman punishes the man by nagging him about some trivial matter. This qualifies as the punishment. The only problem is that the supposed issue that she deems worthy of punishment is a fabricated issue. But is the reward fabricated too? Is there ever really a reward to speak of? That's the trick. The reward is the lack of punishment for the fabricated problem. In other words, the only reward you get is the lack of nagging on a day she decides not to fabricate a problem. This is gaslighting 101. Not to mention, it is also a sign of someone suffering from Narcissistic Personality Disorder (NPD). Due to this unhealthy behavior, you begin to walk on eggshells, and your life becomes miserable.

So, how do we avoid this conditioning and get things back on track? It starts with you establishing an actual reward/punishment system. Not this pseudo-conditioning system that women have created in a desperate attempt to trick men out of their God-given authority. The first thing you need to do is punish her for nagging you in the first place. This establishes you as the authority figure from the start. Shut her down the moment she tries to take the crown. Not acknowledging her complaints will circumvent her false authority. Keep in mind that this is a game of wits. Either she's conditioning you, or you're conditioning her. You would much rather it be you doing the conditioning because you're the benevolent one in the social dynamic. She has neither the compacity nor the desire to be fair. They're just not wired that way. But what does punishment look like? That depends on the woman you're with. Figure out what's most important to her. Whatever that is, take it away until she corrects her behavior. Keep in mind, and this should go without saying, when I say punishment, I'm not talking about physically harming anyone or depriving them of their rights as human beings. (she can exercise all the rights in the world, just exercise them somewhere else). I'm speaking of the things she benefits from because she's with you. A good example of this is attention. If she loves your attention, you can punish her by taking your attention away. Ignore her until she's ready to admit that she's in the wrong.

Or if she likes going on dates or trips, cancel those plans. Or maybe you're the type of guy to buy her nice things. Simply stop buying her nice things. When it comes to punishing a woman for foul behavior, one of your biggest weapons is the word "NO." That word needs to become your best friend. Many of you rarely tell women no. In fact, I'm willing to bet that most of you have never told a woman no. This is the reason why you have no power in the social dynamic. It's also why she's so entitled and emboldened to behave the way she does. This is a serious problem because sometimes you can encounter a woman that would've been a good match for you. However, her last boyfriend never told her no. He literally trained her to be the next guy's problem. Sometimes, women are so far gone that it's not even worth it to try and correct the behavior. As Kenny Rogers would say, "You gotta know when to hold 'em and know when to fold 'em."

Always remember the most valuable thing to a woman is companionship. If she does something unforgivable, the worst thing you can ever do to a woman is leave her. Remember that negative reinforcement is effective when it comes to conditioning, but positive reinforming is actually more powerful. In other words, don't forget to reward good behavior just as much as you punish bad behavior. You must be consistent across the board. Always punish bad behavior regardless of how you feel. The moment you get soft is the moment you've lost. I tell guys all the time that a man is bolder. The moment a woman gets with you, she'll try to move the bolder. If it never moves, she'll eventually stop trying. However, if that bolder moves even one inch, she'll spend the rest of her life pushing it. You have to be firm in your manhood and stand on your principles no matter what. You must create a consequence if you want to see less of a particular behavior. If you want to see more of a particular behavior, you must reward it every time. This is the key to proper conditioning. Some may argue that it's manipulation, but I would disagree. This process creates a functioning, well-rounded relationship, unlike the previous method that women use, which creates a repressed feeling of anger and resentment.

Keep in mind that the punishments and rewards don't have to be big things. It's the little things that shape and mold us over the years. The key is to take the wheel so that you're in control of the interaction between you and your woman. Because if you don't take the incentive to grab that steering wheel, you can bet your bottom dollar that she'll grab that wheel. And when that happens, who the hell knows where the two of you will end up. It's better for you to be the captain of the ship. She can be the navigator or the first mate, but never give her full control of the ship. She'll crash that bitch into an iceberg and then blame you for letting her do it. And don't fall for any shaming tactics. There are those who will call you controlling or even a dictator. Ironically, they won't have a single issue with your woman leading you around by the nose. Ignore these people because they don't have to live with the women you're with. It's better for you to be in control because if anything goes wrong, you will definitely be blamed. I would much rather fail on my terms than crash and burn because someone else is driving the plane.

The bottom line is that in every aspect of society, we have reward/punishment systems. We have a system of rules, laws, and regulations. If we did not have these things in place, our society would fall into chaos. Why should a relationship be any different? Many of us have unruly women because we've never even considered correcting them. We foolishly believe that they will self-regulate their behavior. Society knows better. Her boss at her job knows better. Everyone knows better except you. Anywhere else in her life, she has consequences for her actions. If she cuts up at her job, she's reprimanded or fired. This is why she doesn't do it. If she runs a red light or attacks some random person in the grocery store, she gets a ticket or she's arrested. Which, again, is why she doesn't do it. Take a clue from society and the workforce. Hold your woman accountable. And if she doesn't want to comply...

Fire her ass.

Chapter 8: Standard #5: Absolute Kratocracy

"He who pays the cost gets to be the Boss."

-Unknown

"A man should be able to provide for his family" is a phrase we've all heard before, and it's still widely used in today's society. Whenever somebody says that a man should be a good provider, they usually imply that he should have a good job that will pay well and allow him to support his family with food, shelter, and other necessities.

The understanding of what it means to be a provider is deeply embedded in our culture and in the masculine psyche. Men, in particular, are prone to feelings of worthlessness and depression when they lose their employment and, consequently, their identity as a provider.

Most men will never admit they feel this way, but it is a huge problem. Naturally, men should find fulfillment in being able to provide for themselves, not just others. No man wants to feel worthless, and unfortunately, today's society has a habit of doing just that. Now, the focus is only on what a man can bring to the table.

Traditionally, men and women provided almost equal resources to their tribes in extremely primitive societies; women gathered nuts and seeds while men hunted big wildlife. It's called the division of labor. Throughout most of human history, men and women contributed roughly equal amounts to the family economy. This is why the family unit has been successful for so long. The stay-at-home lady, who lounged around the house while her husband worked outside the home all day, is a relatively new concept in family life.

This idea didn't catch on in the West until the 19th century, and even then, the working husband and stay-at-home wife arrangement were often only open to the wealthy and middle-class. To keep the family stable financially, both men and women had to work in some way in most families.

In today's world, masculinity is directly proportional to the amount of wealth the man is able to accumulate. Let's be honest. His identity is based on his paycheck, at least in theory. Sometimes, this concept becomes very subjective. I've noticed that your lack of wealth is routinely used as a disqualifier. In other words, your masculinity is always judged by what you haven't done or haven't accomplished.

For example, turning your annual salary of 30k into 60k is an accomplishment, but it still isn't six figures. Based on the expectations of today's modern women, there's always a hoop to jump through unless you vet your woman properly, as we discussed previously. Either way, modern women in relationships are not expected to have any mandatory responsibilities, unlike in the past.

Today, women have shamed men into rejecting the idea that men and women have preset gender roles, even though we still expect men to adhere to said gender roles. Now, it's considered shameful or oppressive for men to expect women to engage in "women's work," much less demand it. Plus, women were never expected to be financial earners, which means they were not expected to relinquish those finances to provide for the family.

The only time they're expected to be providers is when they live in a household without a man. This is their little loophole. If there's no man there, they have to be responsible. But only by default. If a man is there, they can choose not to be responsible. In this context, this literally makes a woman's money/ability to earn worthless. This is also why many men have made comparisons between the behaviors of women and children. Women today are like a teenager that has a part-time job. They have money, and if they were on their own, they'd have to spend that money. But when they're not on their own, they want to spend YOUR money and keep THEIRS.

Today's men are considered to be walking, talking ATM machines meant to kick out an endless supply of money whenever women and children need or want something. Modern women are conditioned to believe that even if they earn money, it is still the responsibility of their men to provide for them. Any man who believes this is incorrect (considering how much money women are capable of making today) is considered weak, less of a man, or afraid of responsibility. On the contrary, women are able to completely ignore any and all womanly responsibilities while simultaneously reaping the benefits of a man's provision and success.

According to the findings of a survey, more than a quarter of women stated they would prefer it if their partner paid for everything. MyVoucherCodes.co.uk researched and discovered that 28% of those questioned preferred to be kept a woman. Data showing that 50% of women accepted money for fuel, cell phone bills, and appliance purchases emphasized the necessity for high earners. Almost a third (31%) of married women expect their other half to pay for clothes and visits to the spa. Furthermore, more than half of women (53%) believe their partners should contribute more to home expenses if they earn more than they do.

Based on the modern woman's expectations of masculinity, compared to what she's willing to provide, we can only come to one conclusion: if a man has to have an awesome career that affords him the ability to earn sufficiently more than his peers in order to keep his pockets and bank account flush with cash so that he can provide his wife and children with everything their little heart's desire, then one thing is for sure. That man should control everything. Ultimately, he has paid the cost to be the boss. Because of his blood, sweat, and tears, she (and possibly her children) are able to live a wonderful life. This cannot be ignored or discounted. After all, isn't it the world's standard that only a "real man" is always ready to pay for whatever his lucky lady desires? Considering that most marriages end in divorce due to financial issues, one could argue that making plenty of money is tied directly to the definition of being a "real man." The only question is, why hasn't anyone defined what a "real woman" is?

Whether you accept it or not, the person with the resources is the one who's in control. In other words, the one who has money has the power. And consider the fact that we already established that the woman's money/ability to earn is worthless unless she's alone. Therefore, the proper statement would be: "The MAN with the resources is the one who's in control." Either way you cut it, the man is always in charge because when the man is alone, he's the sole provider, but when he gets into a relationship, he's also expected to be the sole provider. Any other scenario is almost always a detriment to the man. Men are always expected to take the wheel, and those who don't are disrespected and considered weak by society's standards. Think about it. Women are only expected to be adults when they're single. Why do you think they complain about being single all the time? Because being single means they have to face responsibility and take care of themselves—a vexing task for most women.

This is why male dominance or patriarchy should never be viewed as abusive or controlling because the man in the relationship does not impose his resources, provisions, or protection on any woman. It is the women who seek out men with these abilities out of a desire to be provided for and protected. No man of today is begging a woman to take his money or volunteering to sacrifice his life for her. If anything, men are avoided in long-term relationships and marriages like the plague. All the more reason why any man willing to embark on such an endeavor should not only be praised, he should be worshipped. Yes, I said worshipped.

Patriarchal men rarely get worshipped today. Instead, the world goes around bragging about women's sacrifices. Excuse me, what sacrifices? Most men are born with nothing, and many today have absolutely no guidance from the older generations of men. Not to mention the fact that today's men are paying for the sins of their fathers. None of these men inherited a kingdom, only a disorganized feminist mess filled with ungrateful, disloyal females who believe they have the capability of kicking a man's ass. In addition, men have to face the harsh realities of a ruthless world that awaits them when they steps outside their home to earn a living. Opportunities and wealth are not handed to him freely. He must seize it.

No one wants to understand the level of benevolence required for a man to endure all the slings and arrows of the world in order to earn a solid living only to bring it all home to spend entirely on someone else. This is the way it has been since time immemorial. And although it may be your significant other that you're spending on, a man you have the right to spend whatever he earns on himself. Whether it's going on trips, styling in the best attire, or feeding himself his favorite delicacy, however, the man traditionally pushes all these thoughts to the back of his mind and considers the needs of those around him, particularly his family. Then, he makes an active decision to sacrifice his wants and needs to ensure that everyone around him is enjoying a carefree life.

While it is admirable to be the patriarch of your family, it should never come at the cost of your own happiness. If you don't allow yourself to enjoy the fruits of your labor, you'll never achieve your full potential. Where would your motivation come from? If you never enjoy the benefits of your own hard work, you'll never be motivated to reach new levels of success. As a result, you won't force yourself to expand your desires or set new goals. Traditionally, man has always had to sacrifice. This means suppressing what you want and facilitating others. This is what always happens with a man who is in a relationship.

Ultimately, man is always asked to protect and provide for women as if they are helpless children. And in spite of all the strong, independent women talk, women still expect this as well. If you don't provide this, you're not a "real man." And the bitter truth is that all the protection and provision centers around money. Let's be honest. We no longer live in a time where you have to protect women from wild animals or rival tribes physically. In today's time, you can be able to provide all the physical protection in the world, and it still wouldn't be enough. You could be a third-degree black belt with military training and three tours in the theater of war, but without money, you'll be viewed as a loser. Today, your ability to earn money is like your ability to hunt in the past.

A man who isn't able to make a significant living today is the equivalent of a man who couldn't hunt in more primitive times. Today, the richest men are considered the best hunters. Plus, they are the most capable of protecting the women in their lives. Men have to face reality.

Today's masculinity, concern, and love are measured by the money he can spend, just like the food we used to hunt in order to provide for the family so that the relationship could grow and remain healthy. Without money, a beautiful rose can become a thorn in your side for the foreseeable future.

If there is a cost to being the boss in the relationship, the man pays in full. Therefore, the man rightly deserves this position. He has the complete autonomy to shape and mold the relationship the way he desires. There should be no resistance or pushback. His rule should be absolute and unquestioned, considering the significance of his sacrifice, not to mention man's natural qualifications as a leader. Man naturally possesses the tendency to stand by his words. Man is firm and decisive. In most cases, if a man heads a household, the family is well-rounded and in order, as opposed to a female-led house, which is chaotic in most cases.

Any man who takes on the role of a patriarch and decides to marry a well-vetted woman and dedicate himself to that life rightfully deserves respect, honesty, and obedience from his partner. No exceptions.

Any woman who does not accept such an arrangement even when the man is providing 100% is not a suitable wife and should remain single for the rest of her life. The sheer amount of provision that men provide, in addition to the numerous sacrifices men are expected to make, far outweighs anything that modern women of today provide. Based on that logic, no man living by The Angryman Standard should be willing to accept anything less than total and absolute submission. To quote NBA Hall-of-Famer Charles Barkley, "Anything less would be uncivilized."

Conclusion

So, my brothers, friends, colleagues, fathers, and all the masculine men in general (I also include a few of the sensible, traditional women who read this book after a good friend's recommendation), if you have stayed this long and put with me during the course of this book, I sincerely hope that I educated you to the best of my abilities. And just maybe I've given you some hope for the future.

I sincerely hope I also entertained you with my impassioned, engrossing, and (sometimes) galvanizing writing style. With each chapter I wrote, my goal was to pour every ounce of my research and relationship experience into this work. I'm fully aware that some of you may disagree with some of the things I've stated in this book, but that is completely fine by me because I believe logic and reality will always prevail. The good thing about being a man is that we can be swayed by sound logic. (My condolences to women who lack the brain cells or the mental capacity to comprehend objective thought free of emotions and desire.)

Please spread my research and observation to your family and friends if you find it helpful. It is high time that we men seize our spaces from these manipulators and make them exclusive once again. Repressing men by the hand of society (feminism being the main culprit) is genuinely upsetting. Believe me when I say that brainwashing men and turning them into submissive softies is a disservice to civilization. Men of before were busy inventing ground-breaking innovations when women weren't breathing down their necks all day. Today's men are so preoccupied with catering to women, changing their inherent personalities to appease women who only consider them expense-bearing, abuse-taking, pleasure-providing pieces of flesh.

I don't know when the world as we know it will end or if it ever will in the first place. But I can say for certain that if we don't figure out a way to get men back at the helm, we're in for some sad days ahead. My great concern is humankind will not evolve and progress for the foreseeable future if the current status quo remains the same. To loosely translate, if men are told to suppress their innate tendencies and are made to eradicate their nature and natural tendencies because society views them as toxic masculinity, then I think there is no hope for the future. I believe this begins and ends with the family unit, which is why cultivating solid relationships is vital. Our younger generations have all the resources at their disposal. They can change the world, but the lack of true masculinity leaves them with no real mentorship and has them twisting in the wind. Most of these young men who would naturally rise to the occasion have absolutely no clue what it means to be a man, much less a leader of men. These women have left/divorced their fathers and isolated them from all things masculine in order to produce new generations of docile, more subservient men. And it needs to come to a stop. Our civilization depends on it.

But I digress. I've shared enough in this book. Now, bear with me as I end this book with an excellent quote. I couldn't think of a better way to cap off this masterpiece.

"Civilization is not inherited; it has to be learned and earned by each generation anew; if the transmission should be interrupted for one century, civilization would die, and we should be savages again."

— Will Durant, 1885-1981, American historian & philosopher